RECOMMENDATIONS

Sandra Low Mitchell – Well known horsewoman based at her Balcormo Stud

I was too young to know Penny in her pony days, but my Mum can remember going to the boxes parked in a nearby street — out of the box in front came a very small bay pony and little rider who proceeded to win the Juvenile Jumping (as it was referred to on those days!) This was none other than Penny Slack and Hoity Toity who dominated the 12.2hh pony classes in those days.

Moving on to horses and later marrying John Mansfield from Ireland who was to become her great supporter and trainer, Penny was always a force to be reckoned with— she had many forays down South and was successful at The Horse of the Year Show and Hickstead — actually competing in the first ever Hickstead Derby over the course which is still exactly the same as today's event.

Tiffany was one mare belonging to Penny which I particularly loved watching, she was the type that I would have loved to own and ride, they were a tremendous partnership! Penny not only was a very successful show jumping rider but later carved a name for herself as a top breeder of parrots and more recently training and competing with her wonderful Australian Shepherd dog, Roxy, at Crufts in the Scottish International Freestyle.

There is no end to the tales to tell and in later years the Mansfield saga continues with so much success for both Penny's daughter and Granddaughter — But I will leave that now for you to enjoy reading in those wonderful memoirs as told by Penny herself.

Heather Smith – Three times Crufts Champion and International judge

Little did I realise that when I arrived at Penny Mansfield's home around ten years ago that she would take her young Australian Shepherd, Roxy, all the way from a beginner in Dog Dancing (HTM/ Freestyle) to Advanced and onwards to represent Scotland at Crufts.

It all began with regular lessons which were always a highlight of my week, as Penny and Roxy just soaked up everything we worked on. It wasn't long before we were joined by Penny's second Aussie, Flurry, for our weekly lessons and the activities expanded into other events such as Scentwork, Disc Dog and Treiball. So, as well as having Roxy competing at Crufts, Flurry qualified for the UFO World Cup in Throw Disc and Free Disc. To reach the top in one canine discipline in the space of ten years is remarkable but to achieve this in more than one activity is testament to Penny's talent.

It's been a joy to work with such a diligent handler who has such a positive attitude towards her dogs and a talent for achieving what she sets out to do.

Over the years Penny has become more friend than pupil and we have enjoyed many adventures together, from demonstrations at various events to organising planning and fundraising for a team to represent our country at the Open European Championships in Belgium.

Penny has a great sense of humour and is a super storyteller and I am certain that this book will be a great read for any animal lover.

## DEDICATION

To my long-suffering husband, John, who has encouraged me in all my various adventures and has been 'the wind beneath my wings'!

ACKNOWLEDGMENTS

Without Heather Smith's help and encouragement this book would never have come into being and her own book 'Dare's Diary' has served as a very useful template.

My thanks also go to Heather, husband John, and granddaughter, Erin and her husband Greg, for their very much appreciated help in tackling the intricacies of printing, saving us from computer insanity.

Sandra Low-Mitchell and Jackie Storey also played their part by restarting my writing ambitions when they nominated me to write stories on Facebook under the title of 'Life is Good'.

Many thanks to Allan Brown for his Crufts photo on the front cover.

Mention must also be made of my friend, Kareen Tobias, who I often asked for advice or to bounce off ideas.

*CONTENTS*

Above our all-weather arena.

Below our farm house.

## 1. EARLY DAYS

My love of horses was probably inherited from my maternal grandfather who was a very keen horseman. Unfortunately, I never met him as he died before I was born. His favourite horse, Kangaroo, was a winner of many point –to-points and it was a sad day indeed when he was conscripted to join the army and go to war, never to return.

I started riding at the tender age of three when my mother and aunt Flo took me out for hacks on the bridleways around Hazelden Riding School at Mearnskirk, near Glasgow. I spent most of my weekends growing up helping with the horses there while receiving tuition from Mr Robert Young the proprietor. (Many years later I became friendly with his son Billy, and wife Pat, and we even co –owned some showjumpers together). My favourite mount at the time was a little black pony called Smokey and I can still remember the terrible day that Smokey developed bad colic and had to be put down. After that, I rode a variety of ponies and horses, but none ever replaced little Smokey!

All I ever wanted was a pony of my own, but it wasn't until I was ten years old, father relented and bought The Nipper, an elderly cob that was being retired from the riding school. I was so excited and I can remember getting ready for his arrival and making a stable out of old corn bins in our garage. My dreams had finally come true! I soon realised that jumping was my main focus, but Nipper had other ideas! Out hunting he would tackle anything in his path in the thrill of the chase and we would often hack miles to a meet then follow hounds all day and make our way home exhausted at dusk. When the summer came, we hacked to our local show 5 miles away to compete in the jumping competition only to be eliminated at the first brush fence! My disappointment knew no bounds! Eventually, after a couple of years, Nipper was sold on to a lovely home where he spent the remainder of his years in peace and quiet.

His replacement couldn't have been more different in the shape of a fiery little 12.2 hand pony called Hoity Toity. Hoity loved jumping but her brakes didn't work too well! Often when we were practising at home, I wouldn't be able to stop her and she would jump the 4ft iron field gate and take me back home! Our first couple of outings to shows also resulted in us jumping out of the ring, but gradually I managed to gain control and as she never stopped and seldom hit anything, the rosettes began to pile up. By the following year there was no stopping us and we won the Scottish 12.2hand Points Championship as well as being runner-up in the next height group, the 13.2h.h. One memorable moment was winning a prestigious class at the Edinburgh Horse Show and being presented with our trophy by none other than the famous ballerina, Dame Margot Fonteyn!

All good things come to an end and as I soon outgrew Hoity, she too was sold on to the Connelly-Carews in Ireland. It was quite an experience for me as a twelve-year-old when Lord and Lady Carew invited me over to ride Hoity at Dublin Show. The chauffeur met me at the airport and drove me to their ancestral home at Castletown where I spent the night surrounded by suits of armour and imposing portraits of stern looking ancestors! Although, after my time apart from Hoity Toity, things didn't quite go to plan in the ring, it was still an experience to compete in this amazing arena.

Two coloured ponies, Rocky Mountain and Billy Boy, dominated the rest of my career in ponies up until I was sixteen. Rocky won the 14.2 division Points Championship among others, while Billy Boy emerged victorious out of an entry of 120 at Southport Flower Show. Neither my dad, nor my older sister, Valerie, were interested in horses so it was left to mum and I to trail all over the country to shows in our Land Rover and trailer, often sleeping on straw in the trailer overnight. I am just so grateful for the effort my mum made which culminated into a trip to The Horse of the Year Show at Harringay Arena in London. There was no M1 or M6 in these days and the journey used to take us 2 days with us stopping overnight at the Mount Pleasant Hotel in Doncaster where they had stables for the ponies. (It was here, I remember, that I had my first encounter with Henry, the Macaw, who greeted visitors to the hotel. Little did I know then how much parrots would feature in my life in later years).

I can still recall the thrill of competing at the Horse of the Year Show. I remember waiting behind the big red curtains till it was time to enter the brightly lit ring with a myriad of obstacles and a hushed crowd waiting in anticipation. Your name would be up on the big screen and then the bell would ring and you were off!! In this our first visit, but by no means our last, Rocky and I tied 1$^{st}$ in the Junior Trial Stakes and were 6$^{th}$ in the Leading Junior Showjumper of the Year. How proud I was of these rosettes!

Dogs were part of our family for as long as I can remember. Mum used to breed miniature poodles, but it was the standard chocolate one, Topsy, who used to accompany me on adventures as a child. She was so obedient and easy to train and would even jump fences on my command! Dad's favourite was a harlequin Great Dane called Hamlet. Unfortunately, he was hit by a car when he was young, and had to have a steel plate in his hip, which gave him a lot of problems as he grew older.

After my parents moved to the Isle of Man in later years, Mum acquired a little Pug, commonly known as Pugsy, which she absolutely adored. How Pugsy managed to become pregnant was always a mystery as mum maintained her darling would never misbehave!! She only produced one pup which was subsequently named Banger, due to his similarity to a Manx sausage or banger! I can recall one time John and I were visiting and took Banger for a walk on the beach when he did a runner. As we sped after him, shouting his name, a courting couple suddenly popped their heads up from behind the dunes!!

Many other dogs came and went over the years. Tina was one of my favourites. She was a little black and tan mongrel stray that a friend rescued and was looking for a home for her. She was very skittish at first, but gradually came to trust me and never left my side. I was heartbroken when she developed cancer and had to be put down. We had two German Shepherds, Topper and Tara, and a lovely black Shepherd cross called Shona, not to mention the two Akitas, Taz and Mika. Several Jack Russell terriers kept us on our toes and the most gorgeous Husky, Jodie, who was for ever escaping and having to be tracked down at the most inconvenient times! We certainly had a variety of dogs with a Dalmation and Basset Hound also thrown in the mix!

Birds have always fascinated me. When I was about ten, I used to breed fancy pigeons – everything from Fantails to Oriental Frills and Tumblers to Pouters! All went well till someone gave me a pair of racing pigeons. The hen fell victim to a hawk, after which her partner caused mayhem in the loft by pinching everyone else's partner! I tried giving him away but of course, he always returned and I ended up with a whole lot of squabs with grey feathers which no-one wanted!

An African Grey named Coco was my first parrot. He was wild-caught as was the norm then, so it took a lot of patience to finally tame him enough to sit on my shoulder. Later on, when my back became so bad that I couldn't ride any longer and spent a week in hospital and a year wearing a surgical corset and neck collar, the birds were my salvation. It was then I became involved in breeding them in a big way. First it was parakeets and cockatiels and lovebirds, not to mention the fabulous Gouldian finches and other little birds, and then it gradually progressed to parrots themselves. The garden began to disappear under a multitude of aviaries housing exotic pairs. Just as well we had no near neighbours when loud screams and yells signalled 'happy hour' and the approaching dusk.

With the aid of some friends, husband John and I started up a branch of the Parrot Society in Scotland and even travelled to Parrot Conventions in Tenerife and America where we met some amazing people and learned so much about our feathered friends. I wrote articles for bird magazines and even became involved in TV, thanks to David Stewart of Creature Feature. When we finally moved to our farm some twenty years ago, I was hand-rearing fifteen young parrots at the time which all required feeding at different intervals.

Unfortunately, I eventually developed what is known as Bird Keepers Lung, and had to give up my beloved parrots. It was at this stage in my life, nearing my seventies, we acquired our two Australian Shepherd dogs and I took up Agility and Dog Dancing! The following stories recount some of my many adventures with animals.

Smokey

# 2. BANBRIDGE

My dad bought Banbridge for me when I made the transition into adult classes at age seventeen. The horse had done some eventing with his previous owner and was as bold as they come. It was a big step up for me literally as he was over 17 hands, so it took a while to get accustomed to his long stride.

As Banbridge came into his own at the bigger shows, we often based ourselves in the Midlands during the summer with my friend Sarah Jull and her family who lived in a lovely old cottage at Tanworth-in-Arden in Warwickshire. From here we had access to most of the major shows. Sarah helped at me at the events and in return I transported her horse. We had many adventures together including getting the trailer stuck under a garage canopy when we drove in to fill up. The only way it could be extricated was by letting all the tyres down! We were definitely the worse of wear that morning having attended a big party the previous night in Brighton to celebrate Georgina Simpson's (Simpsons of Piccadilly) birthday! It was a very grand affair with several celebrities as well as many of the riders competing at the Brighton Show.

The bigger the course the better Banbridge jumped. He loved Hickstead and we picked up many rosettes from there including a 3rd in the Young Riders Championship of Great Britain behind two well-known riders, Elizabeth Broome and Althea Roger-Smith.

Banbridge and I competed in the first ever British Jumping Derby. What an experience that was with its 22 fences such as the Devil's Dyke, the double of water ditches, not to mention the Table and fearsome Derby Bank where the steep side was being used for the first time. There was an option to come down the Bank or else jump a very tricky stile. As Banbridge was so brave, he gave me the confidence to have a go and even opt to tackle the bank. Perched at the top it just looked like a sheer 12ft drop with a hefty 4ft 6in rail just a couple of strides from the foot. Those that were brave enough to attempt it were presented some cigarettes by the sponsors W.D. & H.O. Wills.

It was a very long way round and by the time we finished I was both mentally and physically exhausted. We finished with a total of 8 faults which was a good enough score to put us in the rosettes. (Over the years there was to be only a handful of clear rounds). One of these mistakes was the silly little 2ft fence on top of the Bank while the other was coming out of the Devil's Dyke. We were very happy to be in the line-up among some famous names!

On one occasion, however, having driven all the way from Glasgow to Brighton with Land Rover and trailer to compete in the Derby, we suffered a mishap the previous night. My friend, Sarah, and I were asleep in the trailer when we felt it move. We both had rollers in our hair so were reluctant to abandon ship. In those days the parking was on a steep incline so before we knew it, we were travelling too fast to jump out. At the foot of the hill was a river so we were rather alarmed to say the least! Luckily for us the trailer collided with a tree on the riverbank and came to a very abrupt stop. I was flung forward and broke my arm but fortunately Sarah was unhurt. I received some funny looks at the hospital when I recounted the story!

David Broome very kindly offered to ride my horse in the Derby Trial Stakes but decided to give the Derby itself a miss as it was hard enough on your own horse never mind a strange mount. The highs and lows of show jumping!

Hickstead's famous bank, David Broome atop.

## 3. HOLLY GOLIGHTLY AND GAIETY

A friend of mine, Tommy Gibson, who was a car dealer but also liked to deal a bit in horses as well, invited me over to see a young black mare that had just arrived at his yard. The mare was about 16 hands and a bit on the plain side but had a kindly head. There was just something about her that I liked, so I paid the £300 he was asking and took her home. She was very green but willing to learn and loved jumping. I named her Holly Golightly after the heroine in the film "Breakfast at Tiffanys". Holly had a very soft mouth and I always rode her in just a rubber snaffle.

It wasn't long before Holly made her debut in the show ring and the rosettes began to pile up as she was so careful that she seldom hit a fence and I don't recall her ever refusing a jump. She did not have the most ability in the world but made up for it with courage and determination! We spent a lot of time down south in the Midlands that year, staying with my friend Sarah Jull, and gaining lots of invaluable experience and even winning and being placed at some of the major shows. We managed to qualify for the Foxhunter Regional Final travelling the 300 miles back home to compete at the Scottish Horse Show held at The Royal Highland Showground at Ingliston. Holly wasn't really built for speed but her three clear rounds that day were enough for her to win and thereby qualify for the final at The Horse of the Year Show as well as upgrade her to Grade A.

The Foxhunter Competition was, and still is, the most prestigious competition in Britain for young horses. It was named after Col Harry Llewellyn's famous Olympic mount, Foxhunter. The final held at Wembley, was always a big occasion attracting large crowds and TV cameras. Much to our delight, we made it through to the jump-off against the well-known rider, Althea Roger-Smith with her horse, Rockwell. Cheered on by an enthusiastic crowd, both horses did their best but both managed to roll a pole and we had to be content with 2nd place due to a slower time. So near and yet so far, but nevertheless I was delighted with my big-hearted little mare!

I felt that Holly had reached her limit and rather than push her bravery to the max, we decided to sell her on to a lovely family in Surrey where the daughter just wanted to compete in a few local shows. We even went to visit her a few years later and were delighted to see her looking fit and well.

Latterly, Holly's travelling companion was a grey mare named Gaiety. As we couldn't afford to buy made showjumpers, our horses mainly fell into two categories. Youngsters we produced ourselves or difficult ones that weren't everybody's cup of tea! Gaiety fell into the second category! Standing barely 15.2 hands but with the heart of a lion, she was an exciting ride to say the least. She would jump anything in front of her but don't try to stop her afterwards! Sometimes I had to jump off at full gallop to get her to come to a standstill!! By this time, my future husband, John, was on the scene and he was always stationed at the gate to clear the way and catch her as she came out! Her other problem was that she was very short striding and had to put extra steps in combinations which could be hairy at times!

I remember one time at Inverary Show where there was a particularly horrible treble with very long distances between the fences. It was causing devastation to most of the class but I was laughing as big scopey Tiffany (who had joined the team by then) made it easily while little Gaiety just popped in extra strides. They were the only clear rounds to divide first place!

Gaiety also won the Northwest of Scotland Championship at Inverness that year and qualified for the Horse of the Year Show. Jumping in the big classes there required a certain amount of bravery from both horse and rider as she put in extra strides in all the doubles and combinations!

We had a friend who was keen to buy her, so she came to try her in our jumping paddock at home. All went well until she tried to stop then found she had to go in ever decreasing circles until someone grabbed the reins! For some reason the buyer decided Gaiety wasn't for her!

Holly Golightly

Gaiety

## 4. STELLA

Stella was one of the most difficult dogs that I have owned. I bought her from a nearby farm that had a litter of pups as a result of an illicit liaison between their Belgian Shepherd and a neighbouring German Shepherd. It was long before crossbreeds became fashionable and I paid the princely sum of £25 for her. A few years earlier, we had owned a lovely black dog called Shona that was a similar cross and I was hoping Stella might follow in her pawprints.

As Stella matured, it was obvious she was of a different ilk. She was so nervous that she spent most of her time cowering under the table. I didn't dare even to take her to puppy classes as I didn't think she would cope with it, so I just worked away on my own teaching her the basic commands. Another of her problems was that she got sick travelling in the car so I would put her in it for short spells when it was stationary. Gradually I started driving a few minutes up the road then take her for a walk which she enjoyed. Slowly the drive was extended but always with a walk for her to look forward to at the end. Before long she was travelling quite happily for a reasonable distance.

We lived on a farm, so she had to get used to the free-range hens, ducks and geese which she loved to chase. As this was not desirable behaviour, I had her on a lead and gave her a sharp reprimand "No!" if she so much as looked their way! We even sat in the henhouse for hours on end until she accepted that our feathered friends were off limits and she earned a treat if she ignored them and listened to me! If my husband John and I had an argument, Stella would take off and hide under a bush or even disappear across the fields to the neighbouring farm where she would be found shivering and shaking in the undergrowth.

Her confidence grew slowly until I felt she could cope with Obedience Classes at our local dog club. She seemed to enjoy working with the other dogs and progressed enough in a beginners class to qualify for the final at the Scottish Kennel Club Show. Unfortunately, on the day, we had to wait around for so long that by the time our turn came she had lost any sparkle and our performance was very mediocre.

I had always fancied Agility, so we decided to give it a go and joined Glennifer Agility Club. At first, she was very cautious about leaving the ground and it took a lot of encouragement to get her to do the dog walk and A frame never mind a seesaw! However, with perseverance she finally negotiated the different obstacles but her real 'bete noir' was the tyre which she had to jump through! It was a bit of a tight fit for a big dog so I couldn't really blame her. After about a year, we decided to make our debut at our first show but as luck would have it, the first fence was the dreaded tyre! As feared, Stella ran under it and we were eliminated!

By this time, Roxy and then Flurry, my two Australian Shepherds, had joined the family and were more amenable to my competitive ambitions. I think Stella probably heaved a sigh of relief as she was allowed to relax and enjoy being a much-loved pet!

Stella

## 5. MY TWO LOVES

I met both the loves of my life about the same time! John was to become my husband while Tiffany was the most brilliant, yet most difficult horse I ever rode! Funnily enough, they both came from the Emerald Isle!!

John, who lived in Coleraine in Northern Ireland and was studying at Auchencruive Agricultural College near Ayr, was up visiting my old friend Tommy Gibson when I just happen to drop in to borrow some clippers. John and I got talking about the forthcoming Grand National. He was going to put bets on some of the Irish runners. Wanting to sound knowledgeable, I disagreed and said the American entry Jay Trump (the only name I could think of) was in with a shout. John laughed as the horse was at long odds but agreed to place the bet for me anyway. As a parting shot, obviously thinking he was pretty safe, he said if it won he would take me out for a meal! Well, you guessed it! Jay Trump romped home the winner and I had my first date with my future husband! I think it was the hat with the peacock feather that he wore to the shows that eventually clinched the deal!!

Formerly named Randlestown Hills, Tiffany came to us as a show hunter from the Hon. Diana Connelly Carew in Ireland. The mare had loads of ability but getting her mind on the job in hand was another matter. She could take any amount of work and John and I spent many long hours working with her wondering if we would ever get her to steady up and concentrate. Gradually things began to fall into place and we started getting clear rounds. She had so much ability that I often put her slightly wrong at easy fences just to get her to try. Clear rounds started to happen as we moved up the grades.

I remember one night coming home late in the dark with Land Rover and trailer and hearing a terrible crash as we took a sharp turn under the railway bridge in Busby. We quickly stopped and jumped out only to find Tiffany and Gaiety in a tangled heap on the floor! As they wouldn't travel with a partition, there was only a bar between them. We quickly let down the ramp and set about trying to extricate first Gaiety and then the larger Tiffany. Our hearts were in our mouth in case they had broken a leg but miraculously they were unscathed with only minor cuts. Some willing bystanders, who had just emerged from the local pub, were only too happy to help by holding the horses while we tried to right the damage. Shortly after this, we invested in a small lorry that was a lot safer for the horses.

One of my most vivid memories was one of the wettest Royal Highland Shows I can ever remember. The mud was so bad in the main arena that the Royal Horse Artillery had to cancel their display as it was too heavy going for the horses pulling the gun carriages. Tiffany coped valiantly with the mud while John and I were drenched through which was no joke as we were sleeping in one of the stables! Everyone was very relieved when the show was finally cancelled!

After a couple of seasons, by which time Tiffany was Grade A, we qualified for the Horse of the Year Show at Wembley. John and I took shifts riding her in before the classes as it took so long to get her mind on the job. It must have worked as she was placed in every class entered including a 4th in the Horse & Hound Cup. She looked so impressive we were besieged with buyers which I hated. I used to duck into the Ladies every time I saw one coming. Unfortunately, we had to keep turning over horses in order to finance our show jumping which was an expensive sport.

Finally, we had an offer that we could not refuse and Tiffany was sold to Mr Cawthraw for top jockey Alan Oliver to ride. I was absolutely heartbroken and cried most of the journey home. I even persuaded my mum to try and buy her back, but it was not to be. Sadly, Alan and Tiffany never hit it off and she was put to stud where she died giving birth to her second foal.

I still have one of her horseshoes which I carried at our wedding and now hangs on the canopy outside our back door at the farm. Some horses just take a bit of your heart with them when they go. Tiffany was one of them.

John and Penny at the Giant's Causeway

Tiffany

## 6. WALT DISNEY AND SHIRALEE

I always had a soft spot for greys and Walter was particularly attractive sporting dapples and a large white patch on his quarters, like something out of a Walt Disney film, hence the name!

I first met Walter in Ireland as a four-year-old, when husband John took me to Knox Boyd's yard. I wasn't too impressed with him at that time as he still had a lot of growing to do and hadn't come to himself yet.

Little did I know that our paths would cross once more a year later when Billy Forsythe brought him over to Scotland and was competing with him in novice classes under the name Dr Zhivago. By this time, he had matured into 17 hands and was looking much more like the job. I persuaded Billy to part with him, changed his named and so our journey began!

Our partnership grew and the following year we won the Scottish Grade C Championship for novice horses. After that, we hit a patch of four faultitis which seemed to last for ages. I was so disillusioned that I decided to sell him and drafted an advert for "Horse & Hound". Walter must have sensed this and from then on jumped at 13 shows without hitting a fence! Needless to say, the ad was torn up and he went on to make it to Grade A.

A couple of years later, while I was in hospital having Holly, John took over the ride on him and my novice, Showtime, chalking up a couple of good wins. One particular victory that John was proud of was against stiff opposition in the Usher/Vaux Tankard which was held at Rouken Glen Park about a mile away from our home. He would come and visit us after the show, parking the horse box outside the hospital and clomping down the ward in full riding regalia much to the amusement of the nurses! John also made the headlines in all the motoring magazines when they published a photo of him jumping Showtime over a Scimitar car!

Walter was a character. One of his quirks was when you tried to mount, he would threaten to rear up when you put your foot in the stirrup. Not funny as he was so big! When he was turned out in the little wood behind our house, he loved to pick up a branch in his mouth and run about like a dog. Also, if you went out to catch him, he liked nothing better than to play hide and seek among the trees!

Combinations were his bogey fence and occasionally he would throw in the towel and then come back out at the next show and sail through it no bother! If he did well, he liked to be rewarded with an ice-cream cone.

We had one very sad event when Walter was turned out for his holidays with a very promising youngster, another grey called McGuire, named after Billy McGuire in Ireland, where we had bought him. It was shortly before Christmas and we were about to bring the horses in for the winter as the weather had turned very cold. As it happened, I went down with a bout of flu, so they were left for a few days longer. A storm blew up during the night and a bit of yew tree was blown into their paddock and when we went to feed them the following morning, I could see a grey shape on the ground. At first, we didn't know which horse it was but on closer inspection, we found McGuire lying dead with Walter standing over him trying to pull him up by his ear. Obviously, the horse must have ingested some of the deadly yew. What a heart-breaking end for such a lovely young horse!

After we sold Walter, I came across him at a show a couple of years later and went to visit him in his stable. As I looked over the door, wondering if he remembered me, he lifted a foreleg, a trick I had taught him many years before. The groom said she had never seen him do that before. After patting him, I left with a lump in my throat.

While Walter was making his way up the ladder, my mainstay was a big chestnut mare, by the name of Shiralee. Probably one of my most prolific winners, together we won the Scottish Ladies, Scottish Open and Puissance Championships. I remember the morning of the Ladies. I had been up all night with toothache and managed to pay a quick visit to the dentist before leaving for the show at Musselburgh. He said the tooth needed to come out but as I had an abscess I couldn't have an injection and if he gave me an anaesthetic I could not drive afterwards. As the pain was driving me mad, I said just take it out anyway! Not to be recommended! Anyway, I managed to drive the lorry and we won the class!

The Puissance took place at the Border Union Show held by the river in the lovely Springwood Park at Kelso. After three rounds and with the wall at 6ft 3ins, we tied first with the well-known rider John Greenwood, father of Julie, who herself became a distinguished horsewoman in later years. One of my best young horses, Power Plus, came from John Greenwood.

Unfortunately, Shiralee sustained an injury which cut short her show jumping career and we sold her as a brood mare to the Low-Mitchells at the well-known Balcormo Stud in Fife.

Walt Disney

enny Slack riding Shiralee at the Bonnyrigg and Lasswade Show, where she won the Scottish Ladies' Championship for jumping.

Shiralee

## 7. JOEY WALKER

Following a phone call from Richard O Grady at Glasgow Zoo, we went to collect an African Grey which had been handed in after his owner died. At the time we tried to match up odd parrots in a breeding program or rehome them as the Zoo did not have the facilities to house unwanted birds. That is how the rather sorry looking Grey in his wee cage came home with us. It soon became obvious that he had not ventured outside his prison for a very long time as he was so institutionalised that no amount of coaxing could persuade him to leave the security of his cage. At last, in desperation to give him some freedom, I dismantled the cage around him and gave him a cardboard box to chew on top of a much larger cage which he had access to when he wanted security.

Initially, he was not too sure about things, but gradually as he settled in, it soon became apparent that he was a brilliant talker and would recite his name and address, as well as numerous other phrases, all delivered in a broad Scottish accent. When we tried to introduce him to a suitable mate, he retreated to his cardboard box muttering, "I got a wee fright!" He obviously had been on his own too long and had no interest in other birds whatever. However, he kept us amused with his antics and commentary. If you got out the biscuit tin he'd pipe up "Do you want a wee biscuit" or "Want a wee cuppa tea?" He seemed to know if I was upset and would come away with "It's all right pet!" "I'll skelp your wee bum!" was another of his pet phrases. When we had friends to visit, they always asked who was in the kitchen when they heard his voice chatting away to himself!! They couldn't believe it was a parrot talking! He might have been a gifted talker but a pet he certainly was not and would give you a vicious nip if you came too close!

All went well until one day I had left Joey on his own for a little while in the kitchen and came in to find he had managed to scramble up some shelves and attack the polystyrene tiles on the ceiling leaving a large crater on the roof and a mountain of snow on the floor!! John came home later that day and was far from amused. He suggested that as Joey had no interest in breeding it might perhaps be a thought to let him go to my friend Ursula Harper, wife of lawyer Ross Harper. She was very into parrots and had two already living the life of Riley. She had met Joey Walker earlier when she came over for tea and said if I ever wanted to part with him, she would love to give him a home.

Reluctantly, I agreed it was probably the best solution, as we already had several pet birds, so I rang Ursula who was delighted and sent over the chauffeur forthwith to collect him. After he departed, I remember hoping that Joey wouldn't lower the tone of any future parties at the Harper household, when he came away with some of his less savoury utterances!

We went to visit Joey in his new home a short time later where, despite having a huge cage at his disposal with a variety of toys, he was happily ensconced in a drawer which he had laid claim to as his own and spent many happy hours there chewing up cardboard boxes! When he saw us, his little head popped up from the drawer and he said, "Did you get a wee fright?

Joey Walker enjoying his favourite pastime.

## 8. THE COWBOY AND THE COMEDIAN AND OTHERS

Never were two horses more aptly named! They were both chestnuts with a white blaze, and they shared the same temperament as well! They both looked so similar, people often got them confused.

The Cowboy came to us from a local dealer with the reputation of having catapulted his rider through a plate glass window and boy could he buck!! However, after our first battle of wills he settled down to the job and won many classes as he seldom hit a fence. After I thought he had mended his ways, he was sold on to a protégé of mine. Unfortunately, he bucked her off and she landed up in hospital for a short spell. I took him back, but he wouldn't put a foot wrong and won his next competition! Undeterred by her past experience, the girl bravely wished to try again. This time he didn't buck her off but just refused to jump, so I took him back to resell him once again and he couldn't put a foot wrong, winning several classes on the trot! Once more he was sold, this time with a warning attached, and fortunately, this time he met his match!

His partner in crime, The Comedian, had a whole repertoire of tricks up his sleeve! He came to us as a part-exchange against a Grade A mare I had called Kos that I didn't really gel with as she made up her own decisions when jumping and would not take direction. However,

Elizabeth Anderson, her new owner, got on like a house on fire with her and had many successes, while we tried to sort out The Comedian and his quirks!

You could be happily hacking down the road when all of a sudden you would be going back the way you came. It was always a challenge at shows to manoeuvre him past the entrance or exit without leaving the ring prematurely!

John was warming him up for me on one occasion while I walked the course at Kilmardinny Show, when they misjudged the practice fence and tripped up. Neither was hurt but John was left sitting on the ground still smoking his pipe! Another time at Morpeth Show in Northumberland, where, after he had won the first two days, we had a Swiss guy very interested in buying him. He came to watch him the third day and wouldn't you know that was the day he started napping at the gate! Needless to say, we never saw the prospective buyer again! He went on to qualify for the Foxhunter Final at the Horse of the Year Show and was finally sold to Sir Hugh Fraser's daughter Patricia.

Around this time, we also had a brilliant, but temperamental, Thoroughbred chestnut mare, Pampero, which on her first outing with me, won the Puissance (high jump) at a local show and also qualified later on for the Midland Bank Novice Championship at Stoneleigh, finishing a respectable 5$^{th}$ in the final. Say No More was another chestnut mare that did well for me and then there was the grey, Peat Smoke, which was sold on to well-known rider, Tony Newbury.

As well as my own horses, I also rode some for Pat and Billy Young at Hazelden Riding Centre, where I spent so much time in my younger days. The best of these was probably a chestnut, Bel Ami, which Billy had bought unbroken and almost impossible to work with. He had been herded onto a lorry to bring him back to Hazelden where he was again driven into a stable where he stood snorting and with the steam rising in the air! Billy spent countless hours working with him as even getting a roller on him was a major effort at the start! By the time I came to ride Bel Ami, all Billy's groundwork paid off and the horse had perfect manners and was a joy to ride. Our time together was short and sweet as the horse jumped so well on one of his first outings at the Butlin Championships at Ayr that he was quickly sold to a buyer from down south.

Mention must also be made of a brilliant little grey mare, Silver Moss, which Billy also bought from Alan Dunlop who had sold him Bel Ami. Again, she was not the easiest and had already the reputation of jumping into the judges' box at one show (luckily no-one was hurt)! Again, Billy's help on the ground was invaluable as he would lunge her for ages before I rode her so that she would get her mind on the job. She was brilliant in speed classes and she too was sold on to John Lanni, after winning a good class at Morpeth. There were quite a few other horses that we owned in a partnership that benefitted us both.

I also inherited the ride on a big, bay, Grade A, Tejeda, that was owned by a Mr Smith in Dundee. The horse was extra careful and had won a lot as a novice but had lost confidence a bit in the bigger classes. He had not the most scope in the world but once he gained confidence with me, he was prepared to give it a go as long as my strides were spot on! I must say it was quite scary jumping round a big course knowing I dare not make the slightest mistake. Our best result was finishing 2nd to Mark Phillips at the Royal Highland Show.

Cowboy

Comedian

# 9. THE TALKING COMPETITION

I can remember back in the days when exotic birds were comparatively rare, we decided to open a branch of the Parrot Society in Scotland. In an effort to spread the word, I came up with the bright idea of holding a talking competition for birds. It was to be held in conjunction with our first sale day in the hall adjacent to Glasgow Zoo where we held out meetings each month. We also decided to have a couple of display aviaries with brightly hued Gouldian Finches and different types of parakeets. We had one member in particular, Andy Moore, who was extremely gifted in arranging colourful displays, and we knew he would come up with something spectacular.

Adverts were posted in the local papers as well as the Parrot Society magazine and excitement spread among the members who were frequently boasting about the vocabulary of their birds and laying bets as to whose bird would be the most talented. Greys and Amazons were the favourites followed by Budgies and Cockatiels. Every owner was confident their pet would reign supreme.

Finally, the day of the competition arrived. The committee members were all up at the crack of dawn getting the hall ready for the big event. My own entrants were Pepe, a Double Yellow-headed Amazon who was a positive chatterbox and would mimic most of my phone conversation, his bye-line being “Hallo sweetheart” with his voice rising to a pitch in the middle. Scarlet, a hen

Eclectus with a rather gruff voice, was my other hope. I might add both these parrots adored my husband who had very little to do with them but only had to walk in the door at night to send them both into raptures and vying for his attention!

Birds came from far and wide. Two African Greys travelled down from Fife with impressive CV's pinned to the front of their cages with more than forty words and phrases. Everything from large, colourful Macaws to little Budgies, had their cages placed in a quiet room in the hall and left to settle down before Richard O'Grady, the Zoo Curator, commenced judging.

In the meantime, the rest of the hall was a flurry of activity. An unbelievable number of people had turned up and many birds were changing hands. After some bartering would come the handshake then a wad of pound notes would appear from an inside pocket and the required number peeled off, both seller and purchaser pleased with the deal.

The display aviaries attracted a great deal of attention with much 'ohing' and 'ahing' over the exotic inmates. The little Gouldian finches were like tiny jewels in an enchanted forest. Most people had never seen anything like them! Members were on hand to impart information on the various birds and answer any questions.

The main attraction of the day was undoubtedly the talking contest and tension grew as the hands reached eleven o'clock and Richard O'Grady himself finally appeared. He slowly made his way past each of the

entrants, stopping in front of each cage assessing the bird while its owner frantically tried to induce the inmate to talk! Anyone that has owned a parrot will sympathise with the situation. Birds that drive their owners nuts because they never shut up, suddenly become dumbstruck at the appearance of a stranger in their midst! Beak after beak remained tightly shut and it was only one little Budgie that finally broke the silence with "Joey's a good boy!" Needless to say, he was crowned the winner and as well as his trophy, received a write-up in Richard O'Grady's Pet Page the following week!

Richard O'Grady swore never again as he lost popularity with all but the Budgie owner. He said it was reminiscent of when James Herriot judged the pets at his local agricultural show!

Pepe

## 10. THE JOYS OF OWNING A BASSET HOUND

The first dogs that I had as my own, rather than family pets, were a liver spotted Dalmation by the name of Samantha and a Basset Hound called Tabitha, named after the TV programme Bewitched which was popular at the time. The magical connection certainly applied to Tabitha who could make food disappear in a jiffy! It was only later I discovered Tabitha meant gazelle-like, which maybe was not so appropriate for a Basset Hound after all! Tabby was the funniest pup and made us laugh when she kept standing on her long ears or getting them covered in food at dinner time!

Both dogs loved travelling to the horse shows with us and had great fun running riot with their pals when we stayed away. I never once witnessed a dog fight even with a surfeit of Jack Russells on the loose! Jack Russells being the in-dog for the show jumping fraternity at that time. One particularly cold night at Barnard Castle show, the dogs proved their worth by acting as hot water bottles. The Basset particularly was just the right shape to snuggle inside your sleeping bag!

I remember one time Tabitha ate a wasp and went to ground in the rose bushes in the back garden before being rushed off to the vet. Another occasion, we held a birthday party for Holly, and while we played games with the children, Tabitha cleared the table of sandwiches and birthday cake, leaving nothing but a pile of crumbs! The hungry children were far from amused come teatime! One tends to forget that while Bassets may be low-slung horizontally, they actually have quite a reach when standing on their hind legs. Also they are quite capable of doing some climbing if there is a nearby piece of furniture to stand on.

Probably Tabitha's most famous and embarrassing escapade was when John and I were asked over to a friend's house for Sunday lunch. While we were outside in the back yard admiring the horses, this vision suddenly appeared out of the back door of a Basset at full speed with ears a-flying and hotly pursued by to two Foxhound pups! On closer inspection, we realised to our horror, she had the Sunday joint clenched firmly in her jaws! After a chase, we managed to corner the thief and retrieve the meat. Our hostess took it remarkably well, popping the meat into a plastic bag and giving it to us to take home for the dogs' dinner, while we sat down to a hastily prepared salad for lunch! I hate to tell you that when we arrived home, John washed the meat thoroughly and we enjoyed it for supper that evening!

My friend, Vivien, also owned a Basset Hound, Floyd, who was well-known to the local shopkeepers in Strathaven. After breakfast, Floyd would often set off for the village heading to the butchers' where he would wait patiently in the queue until it was his turn to receive a tasty morsel. Another of his habits was to visit the rubbish bin outside the chip shop where somehow he managed to end up stuck head first with only his tail in evidence! This by no means deterred him as he waited patiently for a sympathetic passer-by to rescue him!

I still have a soft spot for Basset Hounds, more so when they are owned by somebody else!!

Tabitha and Samantha

## 11. THE TRIP TO KENFIG HILL OR HOW TO BLOW A GASKET!

In all our many journeys with horses, the most eventful had to be when Holly and Lady of Shalot (Polly) were part of the Scottish 12,2h.h. Team to compete in the Home Pony International at Kenfig Hill in Wales.

Neils Christofferson, whose son Erik was travelling reserve, offered to take the majority of the team ponies in his aptly named lorry, Big Bertha. So it was that Neils left Fettercairn, near Aberdeen, at 4am and picked up Polly, the Warnock's Tiny Tim and the Mitchell's Inch High at Strathclyde Park around breakfast time. The Perratts meantime decided to make their own way down with the final member, Jumping Jack Flash.

Just a few miles down the road at Larkhall, Big Bertha blew a cyclinder head gasket. To give Neils credit, he was not long in hiring a substitute box and all the ponies were duly transferred. This was only the start of the problems as the new lorry kept overheating all the way down the road until it too finally blew a cyclinder head gasket and gave up the ghost at the Severn Road Bridge! Meanwhile, those of us who had driven down in our own cars, arrived in Wales at the small hotel and stables, in the middle of nowhere, which was to be our base for the next few days

The Perratts duly arrived and settled in but as time wore on and there was no sign of Neils, the rest of us were beginning to worry. In those days, we did not have the luxury of mobile phones to keep in touch. Finally about 11pm, we received a frantic message from Neils to say he needed help, so John and Davy Mitchell borrowed the Perratt's wagon and set out to the rescue.

By the time they arrived and transferred the ponies yet again, poor Neils was exhausted and climbed up on the bed above the luton for a well-earned snooze. Davy took the wheel and with John navigating, set off back to the stables. Unfortunately, with the strange lorry, Davy managed to miss a gear at one hill, stalling the box so that Neils was catapulted off the luton along with the suitcases and an almighty yell! It took 2 trips with the smaller lorry before all the tired ponies were safely in their stables, by which time it was 1am!

Some of us had already booked rooms in the hotel, but as several of the children had been going to sleep in Big Bertha, it was now apparent that there were not enough rooms to go round. We decided to double up, with even some sleepers on the floor. As the Perratts had beaten the rush, they managed to bag the honeymoon suite which gave rise to some leg-pulling at breakfast the following morning! When asked for our room numbers, we received some odd looks when several folk gave the same one!!

The show itself was located a few miles from where we were staying, so you can imagine the logistical nightmare of ferrying, not only ponies but jockeys as well, to and fro each day. As Chef d'Equipe, I was so proud the following day when our team of Dawn Warnock, Craig Mitchell,

Fraser Perratt and Holly, put all the trauma behind them and finished a very creditable 2nd place in the team event.

John and Davy returned to try and retrieve the hire lorry which had been left lying at a petrol station. As they drove in, a car at the pumps suddenly burst into flames, causing the driver and attendant to hide under the counter in the dubious safety of the office. Davy grabbed a fire extinguisher and pulled the pin, hosing himself in foam from top to toe as he ran to the car. By the time he reached it, the pump had run out of foam! It was left to the fire brigade to turn up and nonchalantly push the blazing car out of harm's way, before dousing it with water.

As the horsebox could not be revived, at the end of the show everyone had to thumb lifts home with the rest of the Scottish contingent.

12.2 hh. Scottish Pony Team with me as

Chef d'Equipe'

## 12. THE TALE OF TINY TIM

Next time you are standing at the ringside at Horse Sales watching some of the rough little ponies go under the auctioneers' hammer and pondering their fate, spare a thought for one such pony – an ordinary little Welsh pony that turned out to be possibly the best 12.2h.h jumping pony in the world.

That fateful day in 1975, the MacKinlay family from Glasgow liked the look of the little 2 year old chestnut colt and paid 45 guineas for him as a companion for their other pony – probably saving him from the knacker. Little did they know that 10 years later he would be in the Personality Parade at the Horse of the Year Show as the reigning National 12.2h.h, champion!

The MacKinlays named their purchase Tiny Tim, and it wasn't long before their daughter, Caroline, had him broken not only to saddle, but harness as well. The local vet was called to geld the little colt but persuaded them to leave him entire as he was so easy to manage.

Caroline soon discovered that Tim enjoyed jumping and would tackle anything put before him. That was till he went to his first show at Foxley Indoor Centre at Mount Vernon where the bold Tim took stage fright and wouldn't go over the first fence! However, things quickly improved and it wasn't long till Caroline and Tim were winning their first rosettes. They qualified to compete in the Small Pony Championship at Stoneleigh but failed to obtain transport to go down south.

In the meantime, the Warnock Family from Chapelton near Strathaven had been on the lookout for a 12.2h.h for their son Iain to ride. They had spotted the little chestnut stallion but thought he was a bit stuffy and wouldn't be fast enough against the clock. Then one day at a show they saw him take off with his rider- who by that time nearly had her feet touching the ground- and gallop past their horsebox at a rate of knots with Caroline vainly trying to stop him! They decided there was more to the pony than met the eye, and without even trying him, Tim was soon purchased and on his way to Mid Shawton Farm!

He was meant to be second string to Ian's other pony, Seaton Bambi, but it wasn't long before he proved a force to be reckoned with and, although only 5 years old, managed to finish 3rd in the Scottish 12.2h.h Points Championship and went one better the following year to become runner-up. One time in a Chase Me Charlie event at Strathclyde Park, Iain and Tim cleared 6ft - an amazing feat for such a small pony and young jockey!

After that Iain moved into 13.2 classes and younger sister, Dawn, took over the ride. By this time Tim had matured considerably, and his sense of humour grew along with his strength, giving Dawn an exciting time at the start as he took the mickey on several occasions! Just as well elder brother was on hand at these times!

In 1980 the Scottish Home International Teams were founded and Dawn and Tim had the distinction of jumping double clears every time they sported the Scottish flag on their saddlecloth. Their first foray to Clewerth Hall caused a sensation when this relatively unknown partnership won the main Championship against all the top ponies. The following season was Dawn's last and this time it was Tiny

Tim's name that was inscribed on the Scottish Points Championship trophy!

After 4 years at Mid Shawton, Tim moved on and this time it was my daughter Holly, who became the new jockey. Even with considerable help from the Warnocks, who knew the pony inside out by this time, it took us quite a while to digest the Tiny Tim instruction manual! After all, how many ponies go faster when you pull the reins and slow up with a kick in the ribs or use of a stick?

As for spurs, you took your life in your hands if you dared to use them!! Tim was extraordinary in that it was usually him that made the decisions and the rider just had to follow. You could see him a few strides out from a fence either lengthening or shortening his stride accordingly, while his 'helicopter' manoeuver came into play if he was too close to a fence! He certainly was unique!! It was difficult for Holly whose other pony, Lady of Shalot, relied completely on her rider, to adapt to Tim, who liked to do things his way!!

However, as the summer progressed and the pile of rosettes grew, we decided to make the trip down to Warwickshire for the £100 Middle of England Championship, a huge prize in those days! Timmy was jumping out of his skin and made it through to the third round when the fences were so enormous that they were bigger than the ponies themselves. It was only Holly and Camille Crow left. Camille was definitely odds-on favourite and went clear in a fast time. We could hardly bear to watch and the excitement was palpable as Holly and Tim entered the ring. With her foot to the floor, Holly set off and Tim pulled out all the stops and much to everyone's amazement beat the time by 5secs! Ted Edgar was heard to comment that day that if he ever found a horse with Tim's ability no-one else would stand a chance!

The next season there was no stopping them and they notched up victories in the Scottish, English and Welsh Championships! By this time Holly was so big on Tim that her feet sometimes hit the pole. It was a sad day indeed when Tim (along with his instruction book!) was sold once again. It was 9 year old Angela Quinn from West Linton that became the lucky new owner. She got to grips with Tim remarkably quickly although there were a few occasions when Tim turned so quickly he lost his pilot! On one notable occasion, at the Lanark Pony International when everyone presumed Tim would go clear, he did so, but minus Angela! This was the 4$^{th}$ successive year that Tim won the Points Trophy with 3 different riders in the saddle!

His fan club even extended across the Irish Sea when Angela and Tim took Ireland by storm, winning both the Millstreet Derby and Irish Grand Prix! The combination also accounted for the Scottish Grand Prix and the coveted 12.2h.h National Championship at Mill Lodge which led to his Wembley appearance in the Personality Parade.

Scottish show jumping lost an amazing pony when Tim took up residence in the Midlands with the Goosen family. This was to be his final home ( although I believe he was leased to the Whittaker family for a while), and after giving his best as always, Tim was retired to stud and lived to a ripe old age after siring a future generation of ponies.

We were just so fortunate to be a part of the legend of Tiny Tim!

Tiny Tim

# 13. BIRDS ON THE BOX

It all started fairly innocuously with a phone call asking if I would be prepared to participate in The Animal Road Show with Sarah Green and Desmond Morris. The instigator of the call being the late Richard O'Grady the curator of Glasgow Zoo, whom I knew quite well through rehoming unwanted parrots. It sounded like fun, so I agreed.

Little did I know what I had let myself in for! When the appointed day arrived, it was like the circus coming to town with vans parked here, there, and everywhere. Cables, lights and reflectors were assembled by an army of electricians and camera men. You would have thought they were about to film an epic instead of a ten-minute slot!

After lots of discussion about how the interview would go, filming duly commenced. I sat with Coco (African Grey) and Skippy (Mealy Amazon) perched on either shoulder, praying they wouldn't take flight, as Sarah Green who was conducting the interview, confessed to a terror of birds flying!

After this, I became identified as The Parrot Lady in the eyes of the local TV and press. With this notoriety came some unexpected phone calls which ranged from a vet wanting to discuss his own pet parrot's malaise to a local primary teacher whose class of eight-year-olds were concerned that their budgie might not be too well. When inquiring what the problem was, she said it was lying on the floor of the cage with its feet in the air! I agreed this was not a good sign and poor Joey had popped his clogs. By this time the children had realised the situation was pretty grim and when one little boy shouted out "Joey's dead" the flood gates opened!!

A short while later, I was invited to appear on Disney Club which was being recorded at the TV studios in Edinburgh. I decided to take some baby African Greys which I was hand-rearing at the time. I was terrified that they might discover their wings before the program took place but luckily, when the time came, they stayed tucked up in their little basin. This was a massive relief when I saw the height of the studio ceiling with its tentacles of wires and other paraphernalia festooned around the beams! Jenny Powell, the presenter, was enchanted with the chicks, who behaved perfectly I might say, while husband John, was even more taken by Jenny Powell!!

About this time, I was approached by Dave Stewart of Creature Feature, an animal agency supplying birds and animals for TV and films. Would I be interested in supplying birds for certain productions?

This is how we came to participate in several episodes of "Dr Findlay's Casebook". Sunny, my African Grey, was the star on these occasions. We spent many hours together between takes with me engrossed in a book and her curled up on my lap fast asleep. I remember one occasion we had to be on set at 9am and having to wait around all day only to be told at 5pm that our scene was cancelled! They say filming is glamorous! Sunny was a marvellous performer and nothing seemed to upset her as long as 'mum' was on hand. She took everything in her stride from being rattled along in her cage on the back seat of Dr Findlay's old car, to being guest of honour at the local church dance. Andrew Cruikshank and Ian Bannen, the stars, could not have been nicer while the food on location was memorable! One of the locations that was used frequently for filming was a farmhouse near Glasgow Airport. Every time a plane took off in a certain direction, filming had to halt because of the noise!

One of the oddest requests we had was for a parrot to perch on the naked 'dead' body of a murder victim in "Taggart". My main worry was that the corpse might suddenly spring to life when the parrot's claws dug into his flesh! In the end, they compromised with Oliver, my Eclectus parrot, sitting beside the body rather than on top! Oliver also added to his credits when he appeared sitting on Gregor Fisher's shoulder in an episode of "The Baldy Man".

These are just some of the adventures we had during our years of filming. Gradually I became interested in breeding parrots, which took up more and more time, so the filming had to come to a halt. Some of my ex-TV stars even went on to become proud parents!

Oliver

## 14. RIDING THE RANGE

It was always a dream of mine when a child, to spend time on a ranch, but it took until I was 65 years old to fulfil that dream. By that time, I had more or less stopped riding altogether due to back problems, but I was not going to let that stop me! We had arranged to go on holiday to Canada with our good friends, John and Jessie Smith, and decided to include a few days stay at a working ranch in Alberta.

When we arrived in Calgary, we were stunned by the majesty of the Rocky Mountains in all their glory. We had hired a 4x4 and the following day set out on the long road to Willow Lane Ranch where we were greeted by Leanne and Keith. I remember the first evening being slightly disappointed at having beef burgers on the menu, but they were so much better than any we had previously tasted!

The next morning, we were assigned horses according to our ability. A lovely little spotted mare called Storm was to be my mount. It took a while to get used to western style riding with long reins in one hand and even longer stirrups. The cinch or girth was never that tight and the saddle had a disconcerting habit of swaying from side to side with your movement!

We would spend the day up in the Porcupine Hills in the foothills of the Rockies, occasionally spotting a bear or an eagle circling overhead in the blue sky! As John and I were the most experienced of the riders, we were allowed to help in rounding up strays or cutting out certain cows. At one point John and his mount had to descend, a hundred foot, steep bank which he swore was as challenging as the Hickstead Bank! The horses were amazing doing most of the work themselves on a loose rein while we sat tight! The ground was riddled with gopher holes and how they managed to avoid putting a foot in one I will never know! I swallowed painkillers by the handful to keep going!!

Heaven help you if you needed the toilet as there wasn't a tree or bush for miles! One poor girl was seen disappearing in the distance on a hopeless mission to find some privacy!! We would enjoy a picnic lunch sitting on the grass with the horses grazing beside us and the backdrop of mountains.

It was an amazing holiday which also included visits to the Calgary Stampede which was on at the time. Every morning there was a free breakfast hosted by a different venue in town. The pancakes with maple syrup were mouth-watering!

We had great fun in a western shop choosing cowboy hats for ourselves before going along to watch the show. It was exciting all right with everything from bucking bulls and horses, to wagon racing and steer roping.

Nearby was the famous Spruce Meadows Arena where many international show jumping events were held. We decided to drive out and see it for ourselves having watched it many a time on T.V. The size of the place was enormous with several different rings, huge barns with stables as well as scores of shops and restaurants. There were free golf buggies for competitors to use to get around. As a show was in progress at the time, we brazened our way past security and joined some of the British riders that we knew for lunch. We even saw Rex Get Busy, a horse we had sold previously, competing in one of the rings!

Our agenda also included trips to Banff and the beautiful Lake Louise, as well as Calgary Zoo and across the prairies to the Badlands where the remains of prehistoric creatures lay. While we were there, Canada Day was celebrated on July 1st with lots of parades, celebrations and fireworks, not to mention Red Indians done up in all their war paint! Certainly a holiday to remember!

John and Penny in the foot hills of the Rockies

## 15. EASY TOUCH

Easy Touch or Mary (the mare!), though only 5 years old, had obviously had a few traumatic experiences before joining us. The dealer that we bought her from in Holland, knew little of her past history. I know when we got her home she was very reluctant to leave the stable and when she did, her whole body was full of nervous tension.

The first year was full of trials and tribulations as we tried to gain her confidence. We began to think that we had made a huge mistake taking her on and would probably have sold her on if anyone was interested.

By the following year Holly and her were starting to click and though they still had bad days, they were getting fewer. Mary was so fast and careful that on her good days she was hard to beat. By the third season, she was a force to be reckoned with, winning countless classes as well as at the Royal Highland Show and a Grand Prix at Fintana in Ireland. She also finished runner-up in the Wembley Ladies Spurs when she was just pipped at the post on the final night. That was the year Mark and their little rescue Jack Russell, Sasha, would have won the Terrier Racing there if only Mark had gone through the finish! Poor Mark had to endure a lot of leg-pulling after that.

We decided to drive home from London through the night, with John and Holly taking turns driving. John took the first shift while Mark and Holly had a well- deserved snooze in the bed on the luton. Halfway up the road, Holly took over the wheel but Mark slept on. As I was pretty tired by this time I climbed up on the luton and crawled into my sleeping bag while Mark slept on. When he finally awoke he let out an almighty yell when he realised his wife had morphed into his mother-in-law!!

After performing creditably in the Queen Elizabeth Cup at the Royal International Show at Hickstead, Holly and Mary were invited to compete in the British team at Budapest and Bratislava. This was a great experience for them. I remember as Holly set out (with Mark beside her) she asked John what road to take out of Scotland! Fortunately, they joined the other team members down south and travelled out in convoy! I think the journey was fairly arduous with mosquitos driving the horses mad and some of the officials at the various Borders being less than helpful. The British team had a win in Bratislava, the first time for many years. When the result was read out over the loudspeaker at Dublin Horse Show, which was on at the time, there was a lot of cheering from the British riders

Another memory which comes to mind was when John and Holly travelled to Belgium to compete. On the way south, it came over the radio that the French port of Calais was blockaded by the fishermen and ships were being rerouted to Zeebrugge in Holland. This was causing enormous tailbacks at Dover. As they left the Dartford Tunnel, John could see lorries double-parked as far as the eye could see so instructed Holly to take a back road into Dover, whereupon John hid in the back while the blonde chick driving was waved straight onto the ferry!

Mark and I flew out to join them in Filou, driving down to the Ardennes in a hire car, and while Mark stayed on site with Holly and the horses, John and I were comfortably ensconced in a beautiful old chateau. We enjoyed a lovely few days before packing up to come home. Again, the homeward journey was threatened by disruption as this time it was the French lorry drivers striking and causing chaos on the roads. The decision was made to leave with the horses in the early hours. Once again, John and Mark swopped places. You can imagine the surprised faces when we came down for breakfast next morning as the guests were obviously wondering how my husband had been replaced overnight by a toy boy!! John and Holly meantime beat the strikers and made it to the ferry without incident.

As Mary grew older, she suffered from arthritis, and although we received several tempting offers, she was the one horse we felt we could never part with. We decided to put her in foal and she produced a couple of nice youngsters including one Hallmark Elite which we sold to Ireland for Dermot Lennon to ride. Elite went on to become one of the top money winners in Europe, resulting in us winning a prestigious Breeders prize.

Third time proved unlucky for Mary as both her and her foal died in tragic circumstances. We were heartbroken and could never face breeding again. Mary was so special and had given us so many fantastic memories, it took a long time for us all to come to terms with her loss.

Easy Touch in the International Ring Hickstead.

## 16. ANYONE FOR TURKEY?

Friends of mine had fallen heir to three turkeys but found their garden was suffering under such heavy artillery! As we lived on a farm, would we consider giving them a new home? Always interested in different varieties of birds, we agreed to give them a go.

The following afternoon a white van rolled up at the door and out stepped my friends, Pat and her son, Paul. In the meantime, I had made a cosy straw bed for the birds in a suitable shed so we reversed the van round and heaved out the monsters. Good grief they had to weigh all of 30lbs! I asked if I should shut the turkeys in for a while until they became accustomed to their new home but was assured that they never went far and would probably stay with the hens and geese in the yard, so I left the door open for them while we went and had some tea.

About half an hour later, I thought I had better check on the newcomers, but the bronze stag and his two white hens were nowhere to be seen. We searched high and low round the farm but not a dicky bird. How could birds that large disappear into thin air in such a short time?

Paul and I bundled into the van and set of up the road towards the next farm. A few hundred yards further on we spotted the runaways doing what can only be described as a fast turkey trot. We managed to head them off with the van and screeched to a halt, jumped out and rugby tackled two of the birds. The only trouble was when I tried to lift my captive to put her in the van, the weight was such that I fell over and couldn't get up again for laughing. Fortunately, Paul came to my rescue and we soon had the three prisoners back under lock and key!

After this experience, I kept the turkeys shut in their shed. By Jove, they couldn't half eat! I never saw feeding hoppers empty so fast in all my life!

After about a week, I decided to give them another chance at freedom, so once more out they came. I kept an eye on them for the first wee while, but after a bit they seemed fairly settled, so I decided to get on with other chores. Big mistake!! When I returned there wasn't a turkey in sight. After about 40 minutes searching, I came upon the trio huddled in a corner at the back of the stables. This game of hide-and-seek continued for the next week or so till I could take it no longer and begged my friends to find another home for them where they could be contained. I must say I was not sorry to see them go as my feeding bill had been escalating rapidly!

If I thought my encounters with turkeys were at an end, I was mistaken. Sometime later we were approached to see if we would consider renting out our disused chicken sheds for – you've guessed it – turkeys. Not just any turkeys mind you, but superior bronze birds. At first it was the breeding stock that arrived as day – old chicks to be cosseted under heat lamps then gradually hardened off as they matured. The laugh came when they decided to move the youngsters from one shed to another. Freedom! The men attempted to herd them, but they took off in all directions disappearing into surrounding bushes and trees, while the men tried valiantly to round them up. Two days later, the last of the escapees were finally run to ground.

As spring grew into summer, the stags were penned off and the real business began! There certainly wasn't a lot of romance in the AI procedure, turkeys being too heavy to mate normally. First the stag was strapped into a 'saddle' where the semen was taken off and dispensed into straws that could be puffed into the hens. I could always tell when the men had been AI-ing as they would come out exhausted and dripping in sweat. It was crucial at this stage to make sure to 'blow' and not 'suck' at the appropriate moment as you can imagine!! After this came the egg collection. No fewer than 1,200 eggs had to be picked each day and sent in crates off to the hatchery.

At the end of the summer the young Christmas turkeys arrived. When they were big enough the birds were let outside to go free-range with an electric fence to keep them from wandering too far. It was priceless to see the horses' reaction to these new neighbours. They would stand in the middle of the field with their tails in the air snorting with indignation, while the turkeys, equally fascinated on the other side of the fence, would stand and stare, gobbling away merrily!

During the Autumn, Mr Fox, having no doubt growing cubs to feed, managed to find his way into one of the sheds and had himself a ball at the expense of no fewer than 20 turkeys. Obviously, he thought all his Christmases had come at once. One can imagine how the word would soon spread to all the foxes in the neighbourhood! Revenge wasn't long in coming in the shape of a jeep full of camouflaged men armed with a spotlight, 'fox' whistle and a high velocity rifle.

As Christmas drew nearer, we had to say good-bye to our turkeys. It was the silence of the turkeys instead of the lambs making me wonder if I could actually face one on my dinner plate on Christmas Day!

Is this turkey really driving our tractor?

# 17. REBEL REX

Holly made her debut in adult classes on the great little Dutch mare Zephyr. Along with Dynamiek, they scored many successful wins in Young Riders classes culminating in a trip to Olympia.

Holly and I had great fun on our horse hunting trips to Holland where we were helped by our great friend, Jacob ter Horst. Rebel Rex, Easy Touch and then Jackpot were all results of these forays.

Rebel was only a 4 year old, barely 16 hands and by the well-known stallion Lucky Boy. He had great ability, but had a lot to learn and tended to make life difficult by messing around and spooking at anything that took his attention. This resulted in a really nasty fall at one early outing at Gleneagles when his attention was taken by some spectators entering the gallery. He lost confidence after this and it took quite a while to get it back again. He was commonly known as 'the Little Shit' as he could have a class nearly won then suddenly nip out at the very last fence!

Rebel was also the reason that Holly and Mark got together. One show at Lethame House, Rebel decided to jump the wrong fence and nearly mowed down Mark who was course building that day! To make amends, Holly offered to take him out for a meal and the rest, as they say, is history!!

However, Rebel did give us one of our proudest moments when competing with the British team in Budapest, he won a speed class out of 150 entrants. Although not very big, he was long striding and ate up the ground and that day no-one could catch him. John, Mark and I were so proud when the British National Anthem was played!

It was certainly an excuse for celebrations that night! The only problem was John was nursing an almighty hangover the following morning when he had to crawl under the lorry in a temperature of 30 degrees to fit a new exhaust pipe. The old one had given up the ghost on the outward journey so we had brought a replacement out with us on the plane. They managed to lose our luggage en route but the exhaust pipe arrived safely. Wrapped up in brown paper it resembled a Bazooka. Was it any wonder we were stopped at Customs on arrival!!

Rebel Rex

## 18. EDWARD AND SOPHIE

I first met Edward, the Blue and Gold Macaw, several years ago when he belonged to Andy Moore, a birdy friend of mine, who hatched him from an egg and hand reared the resulting chick. I used to borrow him when I did talks for some of the local bird clubs as he was a great focal point and so friendly that he got on with everyone, sitting on their shoulder if requested. He was also quite unfazed by different surroundings. One time we were even guests of honour at a Caribbean luncheon and another time his presence was requested at Glasgow Docks when the Tall Ships visited. Edward loved these occasions and was so people friendly, he was a star attraction wherever he went! Gradually I became so attached to him that a price was negotiated and Edward came to live with my husband John and I.

A couple of years later, when we moved to a farm, I decided Edward deserved more scope, so we built a large aviary, 20ft long, 12ft wide and 8ft high. It adjoined a brick shed with roomy living area complete with full spectrum lighting, air purifier and even a radio! Both were furnished with plenty of natural wooden perches and ropes. The only problem was that Edward had had his wings clipped at one point and although now fully flighted he had lost confidence to fly so each day we embarked on flying lessons. I would launch him into the air and gradually he became airborne as his confidence returned.

The next step was to find him a suitable lady companion which finally came in the shape of a young hand reared bird who we named Sophie. How would they take to each other? They politely said "Hello" to each other when placed in cages side by side. Gradually both birds were let out together and in no time at all they were getting on like a house on fire. Now was the time to introduce them to their new home!

Although I now had a pair of Macaws, I was not particularly interested in breeding them knowing it would be difficult finding the right sort of homes for such big birds. I was quite happy watching them from my kitchen window as they played and interacted together, sometimes sharing a chicken bone together or swaying in unison on the swing. Often they would just snuggle up or preen each other in these unreachable spots. Both birds were great talkers and could be heard shouting on my husband or the dogs. Friends often asked who was outside and found it difficult to believe it was birds talking!!

Things progressed happily for a couple of years before I noticed that events were taking an amorous turn and they were obviously looking for a place to nest! Scared that they might lay on the ground outside, we gave in and erected an enormous nest box in the inside flight. It didn't take long for them to claim this as their own and if you went too near it a couple of furious faces would pop up like jack-in-the-boxes!

This was the start of a whole series of infertile clutches which Sophie faithfully incubated while Edward would spend the summer as an egg widower, looking a bit fed-up with his bachelor status. On the third summer that Sophie had laid I could not believe my ears when I heard a squeak coming from the nest box. I immediately started providing them with brown bread and milk liberally laced with egg food, sprouted seed and lots of corn-on-the-cob, all of which were eagerly devoured. Unfortunately, after a couple of days the squeaking ceased and when Sophie finally relinquished the nest box, I found a poor wee dead chick. Obviously it hadn't been fed.

It wasn't long till Sophie laid again which presented me with a real quandary should the chicks hatch. Although I had hand reared many different breeds of parrots over the years, I now suffered from Bird Keeper's Lung and couldn't tolerate any birds in the house. I eventually found someone to hand-rear the chicks only for them to let me down at the last minute. By the end of the summer we had lost 3 more chicks and I was so traumatised by this that I almost sold the parents. However, I couldn't quite bring myself to part with them.

The following year, much to my dismay, Sophie laid again. Four weeks later, I heard the inevitable squeaks but this time they were less frantic or frequent. I kept my fingers crossed as the days passed and I could still hear the odd squeak. It was over a week before I had the chance for a quick look while Sophie took a breath of fresh air, and lo and behold, there were two lovely big chicks with full crops contentedly sleeping!

As the summer progressed, the chicks grew and grew while the parents devoured ever increasing amounts of food which I replenished four times a day. If I was a bit late Edward would hang on the wire and stare at me through the kitchen window urging me to hurry up! Scrambled eggs and corn-on-the cob were the favourites, the latter which I bought by the dozen. I even became quite friendly with the checkout girl at the local supermarket after she discovered the reason for the large amounts of corn I was buying and each week she dutifully inquired about the chicks' progress.

Before I knew, first a beak and then a head would appear out of the nest box until finally the older chick was sitting in front of the nest box, very taken on with itself. A few days later she was joined by her sibling and it wasn't long till they were exploring the inside flight, usually ending up on the floor. I would hoist them back into the nest box at night until they were able to perch on their own.

Finally, the big day arrived when they cautiously followed mum and dad along the tunnel into the outside world – such excitement! Sophie and Edward were obviously on tender hooks as they followed their every move and encouraged them to try out their wings for the first time. After a few crash landings, they eventually made it from one perch to the next. They had got themselves out but would they ever find their way back in again? As dusk fell their parents gave up trying to get the youngsters to follow them inside and disappeared into the shed. Rather than risk them being out all night, we caught the indignant babies up in a net and stuffed them back along the tunnel! After a couple of nights of suffering this indignity they finally followed mum and dad to bed!

I cannot describe the pleasure we enjoyed over the next few weeks watching the little family outside our window. Edward and Sophie were such loving and attentive parents, spending many hours preening their offspring from top to toe. It became increasingly difficult to distinguish the chicks from the parents and as they were eating on their own, I knew the time had come to find suitable homes for them. This was the bit I was dreading. Rather than advertise them, I spread the word among my parrot friends, stressing that a suitable home was of paramount importance. So many people want these fantastic birds but do not have the experience or facilities to accommodate them properly and provide them with the space and attention they need.

The chicks finally went to a chap who had kept birds all his life but whose ambition was to own Blue and Gold Macaws. Being a joiner by trade, he was able to build them a suitable shed and large aviary. Departure day was traumatic for all concerned but the young birds settled down very quickly in their new home and it wasn't long before Sophie and Edward were back into their old routine.

Edward and Sophie

## 19. SOUTH AFRICA

Visiting South Africa was always part of my bucket list. We finally made the trip in the spring of 2009, the catalyst being a request by "Parrots" magazine to write about and photograph the famous free-flight aviary at Birds of Eden.

I was concerned about the long flight as due to my back problems I could not sit for long periods. We booked on Emirates (via Dubai to Johannesburg) as they advertised flat beds. Imagine my consternation when only one out of 4 flights actually delivered and I spent a greater part of the journey lying on the floor! The final hop was to Port Elizabeth where we spent our first night in Africa.

The following morning, we picked up our hire car and made our way to the Kariega Game Reserve on the Bushman River, where we were given a warm welcome and shown to our accommodation in an African-style lodge. We had our first trip that evening with our guide Vynand and 3 fellow guests in a specially adapted safari vehicle. The tracks were unbelievably rough and bumpy a lot of the time but worth the discomfort when we caught sight of our first glimpse of zebra and giraffe grazing contentedly in the distance. As the trip progressed it was amazing to get up close and personal with exotic beasts in their natural habitat – everything from impala to kudu and hippos to rhinos! At one point we were driving along a track when all of a sudden, a herd of elephants blocked our way. Vynand stopped and told us all to stay quiet and still as the enormous beasts lumbered past the truck within touching distance!

By this time night had fallen and we were heading home, very glad of the rugs provided, when a call came in from another ranger to say they had come across some lions. Needless to say, we hastened to the scene to see for ourselves! It was quite unnerving and there was a collective gasp when Vynand's searchlight exposed a large male lion which was literally yards away from us!! He was guarding a lioness and her cubs. We returned the following morning in daylight and sat for ages watching her and the cubs playing. The few days at Kariega whizzed by, sunbathing and swimming in the pool during the day and having a few more safaris in the early morning or at dusk. All too soon, it was time for us to set off on the next stage of our journey.

We retraced our steps to Port Elizabeth where we took the coast road toward the Eastern Cape, stopping for lunch at the wildly beautiful Tsitsikamma National Park, and arriving at our next port of call, the Belvidere Manor Estate, where we had our own little house overlooking Knysna Lagoon.

The highlight of our trip came the next day when we made our way to Birds of Eden which was situated with a backdrop of mountains outside Plettenburg Bay. The sanctuary is the biggest free-flight aviary in the world consisting of over two hectares of mainly indigenous forest incorporating a river and waterfall with the height of the canopy up to 50 metres in places. It took nearly 5 years to build and is now home to over 3000 inhabitants.

John and I were met by Eric, one of the senior keepers, who impressed us with his vast knowledge of all the different birds. We made our way along the elevated wooden walkways which wound for 1.2 kms through the aviary. It was hard to believe we were actually inside an enclosure – it was more like a trek through the forest. We could hardly take our eyes off the many brightly hued inhabitants that flitted overhead. Most of the birds were rescues or donated so were used to human company and would come down to join the visitors and even land on them! There was one little cockatiel that hitched a ride every time he spotted a little grey-haired lady, no doubt reminding him of his previous owner! We also spotted an Eclectus touting for titbits at one of the snack shops. Nice to see that ex-pet birds could still enjoy human interaction if they wished.

We were invited for lunch by one of the directors, ex-pat Trevor Glover, complete with his birdy bag full of treats which he dispensed on the way to the restaurant which sat on an island in the middle of one of the dams. As we crossed the bridge Trevor dashed off suddenly to break up a squabble between a black swan and a white one – a case where apartheid was still evident!!

All too soon, our day in paradise was nearly done, and after buying souvenirs and a few gifts we reluctantly dragged ourselves away!

We spent a couple more days at Knysna which was a lovely little town with a myriad of shops and restaurants lining the seafront, before hitting the road once more.

On the final leg of our trip, we parted company with the coast and headed inland past Oudtshoorn, famous for its ostrich farms. We spent that night in the most luxurious B&B at Swellandam, where we had our own rose-covered cottage with huge double bed and marble bathroom. We continued the following morning into the mountains and finally, via a pass in the magnificent Drakenburgs, making a final dramatic descent into Franschoek. It was almost like coming in to land on an aeroplane, where the whole vista was spread out before us as we rounded a bend, and we had our first glimpse of the winelands. On our way down, we stopped for some lunch in a very unusual restaurant which was situated inside a cave. Franschoek itself was no more than a one-street town surrounded by vineyards on all sides.

Our base for the next few nights was the Franschoek Hotel, built in the Cape Dutch style with a thatched roof. We had a lovely room leading out to a balcony with amazing views of the grounds and the mountains beyond. Again, our dining experience that night was different as we were served in our own little glasshouse in the gardens! It was the perfect spot to recharge our batteries and we made full use of the lovely swimming pool and sunbeds, before continuing on the final leg of our journey to Cape Town.

We stopped en route at Eagle Encounters at Speir where we ate lunch before watching the flying display which featured an enormous Black Eagle and various owls and raptors. It was also a rescue centre for cheetahs so you could watch them being hand fed.

The approach to Cape Town, past the Cape flats, was quite a shock, seeing the tin shacks and level of poverty in which so many people spent their lives, while our first glimpse of Table Mountain seemed surreal, having seen it so often in pictures.

The Victoria and Albert Centre by the waterfront, was every shopaholic's dream with outlets selling all manner of goods. There was nothing you couldn't buy or so it seemed! Restaurants to suit every taste were scattered round the harbour, where one could sit outside enjoying their meal in the sunshine and watching the seals playing around the boats.

As well as taking the requisite cable car up to the top of Table Mountain and marvelling at the panoramic view which included Robben Island where Nelson Mandela was imprisoned, we also made trips to nearby Hout Bay with its glorious beach and seafood restaurants. One day we drove down the Cape Peninsular, past the naval base at Simon's

Town, towards the Cape Point and Boulder Beach, with its resident colony of penguins. It was fascinating to walk along the wooden walkways watching the birds busy with their everyday lives.

All too soon, our holiday of a life came to an end, leaving us with the most fantastic memories which helped pass the long flight back to the UK!

Penguin colony

Cape Town harbour

Birds of Eden free flight enclosure

Happy couple

John and yours truly

We were sitting in a jeep

10 ft. away

Our lodge at the Safari Park.

Cape Town Harbour

Hout Bay

Looking down on Franschock

Cable car to Table Mountain

## 20. FLURRY

Two years after our first Australian Shepherd, Roxy, joined the family, we decided to get her a companion. We had our heart set on another blue merle and even had the name, Flurry, picked out. However, when we eventually went to see the pups, this little tricoloured one made it clear she would be the one coming home with us!

Flurry proved to be a very different kettle of fish from Roxy, who was very laid back. She was slightly timid particularly with strangers, more energetic and loved to bark, but oh such a cuddlebug! She was and is, a fearsome watchdog. It's the one time she can legitimately bark!

Her first trip down South to Blackpool was memorable. We were heading to one of our favourite shows where Roxy was competing in Heelwork to Music. Stopping for lunch en route we discovered that the car boot was flooded due to Flurry chewing through the water carrier! Fortunately, we had some towels with us and managed to mop up the flood!

On our arrival at our rather posh hotel, we decided to give the dogs a leg stretch before checking in. Next thing I knew Flurry had jumped into a filthy pond and emerged covered in a mantle of green slime! We dried her off best as we could before smuggling her into our hotel. Sadly, the stench lasted for quite some time!

Another time when we were away, she manage to get a bit of stick lodged in her throat and it was touch and go as to whether John, my husband, could dislodge it as she panicked and refused to be restrained. Manfully, John persevered and eventually emerged triumphantly with the offending stick albeit with bloody fingers where she had bitten him!!

However, the following year at Blackpool, she managed to redeem herself by winning both Starters Heelwork classes with our Dad's Army routine. My outfit, complete with ginger moustache, was so realistic that on one occasion, one of my friends failed to recognise me. I had tapped her on the shoulder and she was quite indignant when she turned round and saw Captain Mannering! Another of our favourite routines was from Only Fools and Horses with me as Del Boy. Later on, when I was suffering from ill health, she made it up to Intermediate in the expert hands of Heather Smith (3 times Crufts winner).

As well as doing some Obedience, both dogs loved their Agility, as did we! Susan Noble of Red Dog Agility set us on the right path and it was not long before we were out at shows competing. I ran Roxy and John partnered Flurry. If he couldn't keep up with her, she would turn round and bark at him and on one occasion tripped him up so that he fell heavily and bruised his ribs. On another occasion, they were winning the class when John hit the final wing with his hand and down came the fence. We made it up to Grade 3 before John and I decided that it was time for us to hang up our running shoes at the ripe old age of 74!

Flurry really came into her own, however, when she took up Disc with our trainer, Heather Smith. They even gave a demonstration of Free Disc at the Dog Lovers Show at the SECC in Glasgow. Not only that, but at the first ever Scottish Disc Competition in Scotland they qualified for the World Championships in Holland!! She is never happier than leaping into the air to catch the frisbee and race back to Heather with it in her mouth!!

Penny in Dad's Army

Costume

Flurry in the woods

# 21. THE GREAT ESCAPE

While sourcing some more hens to add to our collection, we came across a pair of guinea fowl and decided to buy them as well. It was obvious fairly quickly that they were actually two cock birds and as they were such comics we decided to name them Eric and Ernie. When alarmed they would fly onto the barn roof making a staccato noise like a machine gun! The birds would delight in scaring the wits out of some of the liveries we had at the time. Often the riders were left hanging round the necks of their mounts when they executed a quick about turn!

One snowy winter's night, Eric and Ernie were roosting as usual in the barn where daughter Holly parked her horsebox. Holly had decided to take her two showjumpers to a competition at a local indoor school. She loaded up he horses and away she went while husband John and I settled in with a wee drink for a cosy night by the fire.

A short time later the phone rang. It was Holly not best pleased. "These wretched birds of yours have arrived at the show with me! What am I meant to do?" I could not believe the guinea fowl had travelled to the event, probably hanging on to the roof rack on the lorry roof. They must have been sleeping up there, only to awake to their worst nightmare as they clung on for dear life whizzing down the motorway! I had a momentary vision of them with Biggles-style helmets, scarves and goggles as they sped along!

There was a message over the loudspeaker that whoever has brought these 'turkeys' to the show should remove them forthwith continued Holly. “How am I meant to catch them?” There was no easy answer as guinea fowl are flighty at the best of time and now they would be frightened and disorientated in the dark. “You will just need to try your best” I replied, somewhat unconvincingly.

Sometime later she called back to say her efforts had failed dismally and all that had happened was they had relocated to a neighbouring horsebox roof where they remained till the unsuspecting folk left for home. To make matters worse it had started snowing by then!

I spent a sleepless night pondering upon the fate of Eric and Ernie. Would they have slid off the fibreglass roof of their chosen lorry as it turned out the gate or, much worse, be catapulted through someone’s windscreen causing a pile-up on the motorway? I half expected the police to come banging on our door in the middle of the night!!

The next morning the phone rang once more. “I believe I have some birds of yours” said the caller. Amazingly, Eric and Ernie had endured a trip of some 25 miles back to another stable yard and surprised the owners when they appeared for breakfast at the back door!! As the caller was quite happy to keep them both, we thought that was probably the easiest solution. At Christmas time we received a nice card from ‘the boys’ saying they were having great fun livening things up in their new home!

Eric and Ernie

## 22. FOWL PLAY

When we moved to a farm in the country, it was the chance for me to realise a long-held dream of keeping hens and other farmyard birds. The wooden shed that my husband John had used as a workshop (he now had a much larger building) had been transported with us, and with a few alterations, would serve as an ideal henhouse. John constructed some nest boxes at one end and a couple of roosts and we were all set!

The local newspaper provided us with the name of a poultry dealer, so with great excitement we paid him a visit. He recommended starting off with four Maran pullets and a cockerel we named Maurice. To begin with we erected a wire fence round the shed so the newcomers could get used to their new home and surroundings. After a week or so this was removed and Maurice and the girls were free to explore the farmyard. They played hide and seek among the hay and straw bales, visited the stables much to the horses' interest, but their favourite place had to be the manure heap!! As night fell, they headed back to their shed and with a little encouragement, and greatly to our relief, they were soon tucked in safely for the night!

In the mornings, the birds would all rush out as if they had a bus to catch. That is except for the large Orpingtons who remained on their perches to be lifted carefully down.

If I forgot, they would land with a crash on the floor, often on top of another indignant inmate. If the weather was wet, the leading hens would skid to a halt at the threshold causing the rest to concertina into the back of them. On these days they generally took refuge in the barn. My hens took 'free range' very seriously and would turn up in all sorts of unexpected places. Wanda and Roma, the Black Rocks, seldom missed a chance to come into the kitchen if the back door was left ajar.

Then disaster struck and several hens died for no obvious reason. We concluded that they must have been poisoned and an autopsy revealed traces of horse wormer which they must have ingested via the droppings on the manure heap. Thereafter, when the horses were treated, the hens were kept shut up for a few days till the infected dung was safely gone.

The hen house gradually filled up with all sorts of different breeds including Brahmas, Wyanadottes and spotted Appenzellers. What fun it was building up the collection. Sometimes we went to rare breed sales and bid for some unusual chickens which was quite an excitement. We even took a trip down south to visit The Domestic Fowl Trust to see in the flesh some birds we had previously only seen in pictures. While we were walking round admiring the different varieties, we were attacked by a rogue cockerel that had obviously escaped his run. I tried to fend him off with my handbag, but not before he had torn a hole in John's trousers with his claws.

Our summer social life tended to revolve round when the hens retired for the night. Trying to get them in on a fine summer evening was a major operation as there would be hens everywhere. On occasions we left our daughter to lock them up and more often than not we would receive a frantic phone call halfway through dinner to say one of the hens was missing. If I knew who the culprit was, I could usually guess where she would be hiding! Our granddaughter, Erin, delighted in searching for eggs, and her face would light up if she found a hidden cache behind the straw bales. She loved Maurice as he was so gentle she could pick him up and give him a cuddle, which rather destroyed his street cred with his harem!

## 23. A PRINCE AMONG PARROTS

It was love at first sight! I couldn't believe it! Pip, the beautiful but aloof African Grey hen that had turned her beak up at various suitors, was in a frenzy of excitement at the arrival of the newcomer. The object of her desire was a rather nondescript Grey with a devil-may-care attitude, going by the name of Prince. He had come to us via the late Richard O'Grady, curator of Glasgow Zoo. The phone call had been short and to the point. "Come and fetch this bird before it wrecks my office!" We had an arrangement with the Zoo whereby any unwanted parrots were either rehomed or, whenever possible, set up in a breeding situation.

Anyway, back to the story! We decided to risk letting the two birds out together in the same room. So, with towel in one hand - in case of emergency- we opened the cage doors and stood back to see what would happen. Often these arranged marriages can go horribly wrong with blood and feathers flying! Prince flew immediately onto Pip's cage and the two started 'beaking' right away. It wasn't long before the pair were into heavy petting and within half an hour they were treading! From then on, the pair were inseparable, so a few days later I transferred them into an aviary with a nest box. Before long, Pip laid a clutch of eggs while Prince assumed sentry duty at the entrance to the nest box. We thought that as this was a first attempt the eggs might be infertile, but no, three healthy chicks emerged – bang on cue!

Prince turned out to be an excellent father keeping Pip and the chicks well – fed and guarding them with his life. Bringing them in for hand-rearing at three weeks old proved to be a major operation, as Prince defended them beak and nail. We felt badly about it and decided next time we would let them parent rear. The first batch we wanted to hand feed as Pip had come to us from some friends in Edinburgh on the understanding that if she bred, they would get a hand- reared chick (which make better pets) in return. Needless to say, they were delighted at the outcome!

In the two decades that Pip and Prince were together, they produced countless chicks. Some went as pets, while others we retained as breeding stock for the future. Many were brilliant talkers, as mum and dad started lessons early, by conversing with them in the nest box. Pip and Prince were soulmates. Often you would see them contentedly sitting, preening each other in the early morning sunshine.

Then the unthinkable happened! I was feeding the birds one morning when I noticed Pip looking rather unsteady on her perch. Immediately I fetched a towel and caught her up, only – to my horror – have her die in my arms a few minutes later. The post-mortem showed she had suffered a heart attack. Prince was inconsolable and sat in a dejected heap. No longer did we get greeted with a cheery 'Good morning' when we passed his flight.

I was in a quandary as to what to do. Would Prince ever take to another mate after losing the love of his life? I couldn't bear to see him look so unhappy, so eventually decided to look for another partner for him. With this in mind, I asked some friends who were going to a Sale if they could look out for a suitable hen.

After receiving a phone call from them a few days later, I couldn't wait to drive over to their house to see the new addition. Proudly, they lifted the cover off the Grey's cage to reveal the big, beautiful bird inside. The only problem was it had a black sexing ring on the right leg which generally denotes a cock bird! "Did you get a sexing certificate?" I asked my friend Paul. "No need" he replied, "the gentleman who sold it seemed very genuine and assured me it was a hen!" What could I say? I took the bird home and immediately arranged for a DNA test. Lo and behold, a couple of weeks later, it came back saying that it was indeed a hen!

Once the parrot, called Paula - after my friend – had had time to settle in, I moved her and Prince into a spare flight and watched anxiously to see what the reaction would be. Prince immediately rushed over, obviously thinking Pip had returned, but on realising his mistake a look of disgust came over his face and he retreated woefully to the far end of the perch.

Weeks turned into months with the two birds completely ignoring each other. Just when I was wondering what to do next, I noticed at last they were interacting and finally sitting together. Obviously, the period of mourning was over. Hopefully, I put in a nest box and it wasn't too long before they were both inspecting it. Shortly afterwards, Paula laid and duly hatched three big chicks. Prince was back to his usual cheery self and threw himself with gusto into rearing the chicks.

Like all good love stories, this one had a happy ending. Paula and Prince settled comfortably into married life and produced many chicks and even grandchicks.

Prince

## 24. COUNTDOWN TO CRUFTS

Most folk in the competitive dog world, whether it be showing, agility or whatever, have a trip to Crufts as their eventual goal. I can honestly say that when I started HTM, or Dog Dancing, at the ripe old age of 70, it never crossed my mind. It started out as a bit of fun to have with my Australian Shepherd, Roxy.

As a youngster Roxy had slipped on some ice and broken her front leg so badly in 3 places that she had to have a metal pin inserted. For months we didn't know if she would recover sufficiently to walk without a limp. Thankfully, due to luck and the surgeon's skill, she made a complete recovery.

Despite this shaky start and my bad back and thanks to all the help and encouragement from my friend and trainer, Heather Smith (triple Crufts winner), 3 years later we reached the dizzy heights of advanced in Freestyle. When we just missed qualifying for the semi-finals for Crufts, I was disappointed but not heartbroken. However, sometimes fate can play funny tricks!

Late one autumn night, we received a phone call from Gina Pink (who organised the HTM at Crufts) saying that one of the dogs that had beaten us in the Qualifier had sadly died. As we were next in line, would we like to take its place in the Semis and also represent Scotland in the International Freestyle at Crufts? (Heather Smith was the only other

Scottish competitor to qualify that year but judging commitments made it impossible for her to compete.) To say we were taken aback was an understatement! Were we really up to performing on the green carpet in front of thousands of people?

A very sleepless night followed as Gina required an answer by the following morning. Half of me wanted to rise to the challenge while the other half thought we might not be good enough and stick out like a sore thumb in such elite company! After a hurried discussion with Heather, we decided to give it a go. After all, nothing venture nothing gained! A few months of hard work lay ahead with the Semis in January and Crufts at the beginning of March.

The routine we were working on was from Fawlty Towers. The music didn't alter much all the way through, so I had to listen for any nuances as to what move or trick was required at that particular point. It is essential to know where you are in the routine and whether to hurry up or slowdown in order to finish in time to the music. Sometimes your dog has its own ideas and does not always respond to the cues at the exact moment which doesn't help! Only when you know the routine and music inside out and the dog knows all the moves and tricks, do you try and put the whole thing together. Sometimes it can take a year to perfect a routine!!

I was lucky to have help from not only Heather, but also dance teacher Marylin Killen. The maestro himself, Attila

Szkukalek, happened to be staying with us while he held a course in Scotland. His input was also greatly appreciated.

Towards the end of January, we made a trip down to Rugby in Warwickshire for the Semis. It was not our best performance as we had changed the ending at the last minute, somewhat confusing Roxy. It certainly didn't help my confidence for Crufts which was just over a month away.

Any mistakes we had at the Semis were hopefully ironed out before the trip to Crufts. All too soon, we were packing the car with not only our suitcases but props as well. The latter included a table and armchair among other things and of course, my waiters outfit. Last, but not least, the dogs and all their accoutrements were loaded. The car was full to bursting as we set off on the drive down to Birmingham where we were booked into a hotel near the National Exhibition Centre. On our arrival, the dogs were treated like VIPs and had their own bowls and biscuits waiting in the hotel room.

When the Big Day dawned, we set out early for the NEC. My main worry was how we were going to transport all our equipment from the car park which was a considerable distance from the main Hall. I had contacted the Kennel Club to get special dispensation for us two pensioners to unload our props at the door of the Hall, but unfortunately no reply was forthcoming. My worst fears were realised when we arrived and had to park half a mile away. How on earth were we going to transport everything when my bad back prevented me from helping? Valiantly John set out with a folding table and armchair in one hand and several bags under the other while I carried the basket of food and had Roxy on her lead.

Everywhere we looked there were people and dogs of all kinds making their way like pilgrims towards the Hall. We queued for a shuttle bus and just as John struggled aboard, I flagged down a taxi which I thought might make things easier. As the bus doors were closing, John jumped up and asked to be let off again! A verbal barrage then ensued before the driver reluctantly opened the doors. Meantime the taxi driver spotting John laden down with luggage, promptly stepped on the gas and drove off! Eating a lot of humble pie and with our tails between our legs, we managed to reboard the bus, incurring several dirty looks in the process. Our stress levels by this time were through the roof!!

Fortunately, by the time we had struggled through the crowds in the Hall to find our designated area, I had a couple of hours to calm down. Meantime poor John had enlisted the help of a friend to bring the rest of the stuff from the car. As is the custom in International competition, presents and good luck cards were exchanged with the other competitors from around the world. I was overwhelmed by the gifts and mementoes that came our way!

Finally it was time to go to the changing room and get into my waiter's costume. There was no going back now! As the countdown began, we were ushered through the enormous crowd to the inner sanctum outside the main arena. I was to be the first competitor but had little chance to warm up Roxy as the Flyball teams had just exited the ring and were taking up most of the space! Before I knew it, our props had been taken into the ring as Roxy and I waited in the wings! Our moment in the spotlight had arrived! As we entered the famous arena, the commentator, Dave Ray, called out our names while I just prayed Roxy wouldn't get stage fright under the bright lights and with 4,000 spectators watching!

The music started and Roxy did her send away across the arena and jumped up on her chair, ringing her bell for service! The next four minutes passed in a dream and Roxy rose to the occasion, following all my cues. It went better than I could have ever imagined! I was buzzing as we left the ring to much applause and I was just so grateful to Roxy for rising to the occasion! We watched the rest of the competition and were enthralled by many of the performances, particularly the winner Lucka Plevova and her dog, Jump, representing Japan. We finished 12$^{th}$ out of 15 and I was delighted with the result in such illustrious company. The resultant rosette was one I will always cherish.

It turned out that this was one of our last performances as ill health caught up with me shortly afterwards. At least I could treasure the memory of Roxy and I representing Scotland at Crufts!!

International competitors exchange presents.

International Ring Crufts, Roxy and her rosette.

The bounty of presents from the competitors

Roxy with her rosette

## 25. JACKPOT

On one of our horse-hunting trips to Holland, our friend Jacob ter Horst had taken us to see a magnificent, 4-year-old, chestnut stallion owned by a friend of his, Tony Hasselback. I must admit I fell in love with the horse at first sight but had my doubts as to whether he would be too much horse for Holly at the stage she was at. However, I decide to take the chance of buying him, although it was the most I had ever paid for a horse. When I told John on the phone, he thought I was talking guilders which would have been considerably less! Due to a few complications when importing a stallion, we decided to have him gelded before he left Holland.

As I had anticipated, Jack was quite a handful for Holly as he stood 16.3 hands and was powerfully built and also quite sensitive in temperament. It was the start of a long arduous road. The first glimpse of light at the end of the tunnel was the following year when we took him over to Cavan in Ireland for the Five-Year-Old Championship. Both Holly and Jack were in great form and produced three fabulous clears over enormous fences to finish a very creditable 3$^{rd}$ place in a very high-class field. It is worth noting that the first three prize winners all went on to compete internationally. Later that year, while Holly was abroad with the British team, Sandra Low-Mitchell took over the ride and piloted Jack to victory in the Newcomers Regional Final, thereby qualifying for the final at Wembley.

By Holly and Jack's third season together, things finally fell into place. They jumped well at Royal Windsor followed up by a win in the Grand Prix at Southview in Cheshire. By this time, we were getting a lot of interest from buyers. It was Robert Smith who persuaded Norman del Joio to fly over from the United States to try Jack. Norman was so impressed with the horse that he put together a syndicate to buy him. As we were gearing up for the Royal Highland Show, we were asked to get Jack vetted. No problem we thought, until we heard we had to go all the way to Newmarket to get it done!

Holly and Jack went to stay with Robert Smith to await the deal being finalised and Jack's flight to America. We were slightly apprehensive as Jack was such a fidget in the horsebox. He would batter hell out of the lorry if it was held up at lights or an Orange Parade! As far as I know though, everything went smoothly on the plane.

Norman and Glasgow, (where we lived then) as he was renamed, formed a great partnership. They made a return visit to Britain to capture the King George V Cup at the Royal International Horse Show at Hickstead, then went on to become leading money winners for a time in the States. Jack was finally retired to live out his days on a ranch owned by one of the syndicates.

Jack's legacy to our family was to help give us the wherewithal to purchase the farm where we all live today.

John and I are blessed to still be involved with horses, albeit to a much lesser extent.

Nowadays, activities mainly centre around Codie. At the tender age of fourteen years old, she is already making her mark in adult classes with her youngsters, Ciska and the brilliant little stallion, Kasper. She is lucky to be helped and guided by Holly and Mark (now an International Course Designer) and have all the facilities on hand. Here's to the future!

Daughter Holly riding Jackpot

## ABOUT THE AUTHOR

Penny's first love was horses and show jumping. She produced them from complete novices, often to top class and even international standard. Along the way she competed in the first Hickstead Jumping Derby and the Horse of the Year show many times. Her daughter, Holly, and now her granddaughter, Codie, are carrying on the family tradition and have also achieved great jumping success, while son-in-law Mark, is an International Course Builder.

Feathered creatures held a fascination for Penny which started with breeding pigeons and moved on to parakeets and parrots. This saw her start a branch of the Parrot Society in Scotland and also become involved in rehoming unwanted parrots. Television appearances followed with Disney Club and The Animal Road Show while also providing parrots for Dr Findlay, Taggart and The Baldy Man and several other programmes. When Penny and husband John, along with Holly and Mark, moved to a farm, she realised a dream of breeding horses as well as keeping all sorts of different birds and poultry.

As a free-lance writer, Penny has had many articles and interviews published in Horse and Hound and The Scotsman etc. even venturing as far afield as Holland and

South Africa to cover stories for Parrots International magazine.

Latterly dogs took centre stage when two Australian Shepherds, Roxy and Flurry, joined the family, and set Penny some new challenges in Obedience, Agility and Heelwork to Music. Roxy, in particular, rose to the occasion and helped Penny represent Scotland in the International Freestyle Dog Dancing competition on the green carpet at Crufts.

Her husband, John, who accompanied her in all these animal adventures, said there was never a dull moment!

Penny with Skippy and Coco

Printed in Great Britain
by Amazon

71263772R00068